One can find so many pains when the rain is falling.

– John Steinbeck

contingency plans

poems

d a v i d   k .   w h e e l e r

ts T. S. Poetry Press • New York

T. S. Poetry Press
Ossining, New York
Tspoetry.com

Throughout this collection, various pieces include references to the following brands and sources: Lucky Strike is a product of Reynolds American Inc.; "Sound & Vision" is from the album *Low* by David Bowie, RCA Records; "This is the First Day of My Life" is from the album *I'm Wide Awake, It's Morning* by Bright Eyes, Saddle Creek Records; *Wilby Wonderful* is a film by Daniel MacIvor, Mongrel Media; *My Super-Sweet Sixteen* is an MTV program; *Shark Week* is a Discovery Channel series; Pabst Blue Ribbon is a product of Pabst Brewing Company; *The New York Times* is a product of the New York Times Company; VHS is a product of JVC.

Cover image by Kelly Langner Sauer. kellylangnersauer.com

ISBN 978-09845531-2-9

Library of Congress Cataloging-in-Publication Data:
Wheeler, David K.
    [Poems.]
    Contingency Plans: poems/David K. Wheeler
    ISBN 978-09845531-2-9
    Library of Congress Control Number: 2010937840

The author and publisher wish to express their grateful acknowledgment to the following publications and venues in which these poems and essays first appeared:

Jeopardy Magazine: I have nothing memorized, Because I speak on my feet, The Chimera, Sunday Morning Bread, Conversation Piece. *The Penwood Review:* Christmas Morning. *Chronogram Magazine:* Your Bright Wounds. *International Arts Movement.org:* On Restlessness. *TheHighCalling.org:* Walking the Line Backward and Forward.

to Dad, to Mom, to Dan

Contents

IV. Walking the Line Backward and Forward

V. Sanctuary

I.

Form

We're sitting on the patio, Lu and her husband Norm, and I, outside a coffee pub in Moscow, one of the twin college towns straddling the Idaho-Washington border. I've come to visit friends I have not seen in years, and to stretch my legs. I must be drinking ale while we traipse around topics like literature and philosophy in the healthy hours of the evening.

"You studied creative writing?" Norm asks me. "What do you write?"

He and I are meeting for the first time, and I am the type to feel a need to prove to spouses of friends I have known since grade school that I am not a chump; so, with squinted eyes and syrupy tone I say, "Personal essays, lately; but, I've been writing poetry longer than that. I sort of move in seasons: I'll write essays for a while, then fiction, then poetry," and I try to shift the conversation to comparisons between modern transgression fiction and the later works of C. S. Lewis.

Norm persists on the topic of poetry and the three of us spend the next hour considering form and image, diction and meter. His manner challenges me to keep up in ways I am not used to. Even writers workshops during my undergrad weren't quite as aerobic as this after-dinner conversation between cigars. Lu tells me later, "Norm wasn't arguing with you, you know. He just gets excited about poetry."

"I know," I say. "I'm easily on the defensive."

I've been reading the poet Kathleen Norris, and in her memoir, *The Cloister Walk*, she suggests that, for better or worse, poetry might best resemble faith when considering all the strict technicality and consequential insecurities. The great poets know about forms and structures, but also the space within the structure for play, exploration, mistakes, and—perhaps most important—creativity. But, lately, in classrooms where poetry is taught and hammered and memorized, the forms have transformed into dogma. The question Norris poses is whether or not we have done the same to faith.

Volatile, maybe, a suggestion; but it resonates with honesty I admire. Just as I struggle to keep up with poetry, I struggle to keep up with faith. But I find grace in their pairing. If in one I fall short—and often I do—I find grace in the other, in much the same way I am beginning to realize that my shortcomings in this life might find grace in the next. When I am petty, argumentative, and selfish; hurtful and injured; lonely and worrisome, grace is manifest in the resulting poetry. And when I write badly, when I get it wrong, and when the forms fall apart; I know there is grace in faith—faith that is practiced, faith that is vulnerable and defenseless because it transcends form and structure.

When I say I write in seasons—essays in one, poems in another, and fiction somewhere along the way—I mean that I am trying every door to a sanctuary to which I convince myself others have already found access. What I fail to realize is that we all search, and we must appreciate the process, the challenges, until that which is perfect has come and we see face to face (1 Corinthians 13:12). My hope is that my poetry serves as a temporary testament to how grace has made right what I have gotten wrong.

11 Demerits

One
for every day I am
late   use   profanity
sleep past ten AM
or stay up until

two   watching MTV's
Super-Sweet Sixteen
reruns from *Shark Week*
or anything on sixty-

three
snoring too loudly at

four
drinking too much
Pabst   canned or tapped
it doesn't matter.

Five   for dirty
dishes   jokes   clothes
and phone calls
lasting more than
half an hour with

six
minutes of humming

seven
or more misunderstood
pop culture references or

eight flirtations

nine   year olds
could come up with.

          Ten
for lies   nail biting
knuckle popping   whining
pity   party   hopping
not running   not writing
and listening to music
louder than

eleven   on the dial
snubbing vagrants
and drinking more
than a French press alone.

Midnight Screening

Dull night like this and I
am at the video store for
low budget independents
that wouldn't interest
me if not for insomnia and
a little too much skin.

It's late and I might wait
too long for the right one
considering its only function
is putting me to bed.

Strange how tame I am
here, the clerk about his
business, God knows
what else he does when
he's not stamping my
frequent renter card or
filing titles back where
they belong; and, I am
free to browse in peace
I hope to bring home
for a night of easy sleep.

Across the street there
are Tuesday night bars
open for shows I won't
go to for no reason and
would find reasons not
to, even on prime nights.

The pale fluorescent light
inside dawns on floorboards
that creak between S and
T, and the VHS collection
with foam inserts where
tapes once were kept before
they were stored behind
the clerk's corner counter.

He closes at midnight and
I find *Wilby Wonderful* by 11:39.

ID, cash, stamp card, receipt,
back to my car on the street
knowing I can't just keep
renting movies when I
can't get to sleep because
they serve to keep me up
until they're over, while
the night is slipping

beneath my sheets.

Take Shelter, Take Cover

Seclusion
is a man refusing to revolve the doorway.
He pushes supermarket grocery carts
and avoids getting involved with anyone.
Loaded with bottled water and resolution,
he resides in the stale firmament
occupied by everyone
he never looked in the eye.
Between aisles of cold metal shelves
he carts just enough to horde
himself, a causation of solitude,
like how ipecac induces vomiting,
with weak corners of his mouth.
Butterflies are moths to him;
growing up was never metamorphosis,
merely a string of days leading to the present.
Through the revolving door,
there is an ocean in the air.
He'll just wait it out.

Still,
he is not what you would expect
as he watches clouds travel from his doorstep.
He'll close his eyes and think of record players,
his table turning to static,
distorted warbles of misunderstood memoir,
circling in toward another night alone.
Beneath the storm cellar doors,
a light bulb hangs from a thread
above aluminum shelves of aluminum cans.
Outside exist networks of cables
and wires and telephone lines:
people linked to people linked to people.
He is not; but, he
acquires

messages in morning mirror fog.
They are slender-lettered fingers
reaching down his throat for words
he never could choke out—
pulled up in unfamiliarity and aphasia,
opaque, like déjà vu.
Like a ghost struggling from tangled strings
attached to everything he's fallen for.

Before you discovered a gift in thievery

I relocated my heart from my sleeve
to an unmarked envelope in my back pocket.

When I said, *You look nice today*
I never wanted you to think otherwise.

You're sure I invent reasons to see you
but pretend not to know the difference.

The corners of our mouths are curtains
that reveal the space behind our ribs
with a smile when we lack the guts to speak.

Your Bright Wounds

So this is how you nurse your brightest wounds,
when all your bruises bulge like botulin
beneath a field of skin as thin as tin
that's stretched so tightly and so absolute.
Your scabs, in baths of balmy solutes, soon
grow soft as water leeches gently in.
The woven threads of soiled bandaging
are wads of tenderness, discarded too.
Between the sticks, the grist, and gravel bits
that nestle far below your shiny scars
and fester long beyond their time to heal,
the memories that breed in muscles twist
your sinews 'round your veins until your heart
is split and every stitch forgets to feel.

The Chance of Rain

When it rains here, we soak
up to our ankles and down
from our hoods. You wouldn't
believe all the water teeming
in the cracks of our streets and
sliding down the sidewalks
in thin, fleeting sheets. We
could almost be swept away.

Contingency Plans

If we might figure out why the water waits
If we could reason our way out of this mess,

> Then we might never have reason to fear hurricanes.
> Then we could clean the cellar, closets, and the garage.

When we manage to stitch the night by all its stars,
When we finally think of names for everyone,

> Make sure to keep the knot from slipping out of sight.
> Make sure to tell each, *I love you, I love you, I love you.*

Suppose we try returning to times when God was God,
Suppose we decide our recycling ranks next to holiness,

> And I will never yield the floor for pleas for mercy.
> And I will try to keep the bins kempt and orderly.

Forecast

Hard to say if anyone expected the torrent, how it
showed up overnight, like the flu. They say grace is like that, like
    rain. Maybe
because they both come at no one's behest: Heaven just about its
    business, shedding sheets of
love, water, blessing. The only thing about it is duration, when
    the shower won't let up
and everything soaks through. Fabric starts to smell or the
    basement floods. It all gets
musty, moldy. It's partial to suppose this life, graced, is changed
    enough, like that's the
whole of it. Not wrung, nor washed.

Photograph, 1993

The sky grows brighter
almost white
as though the day has been
overexposed, and the cobalt house
across the street moirés.
The record skips.
Amber-skinned children
run a hose; and, their mother,
whose hair embarrasses her,
suns nearby, with dad
mowing grass beside the drive.

II.

Lake Padden, Bellingham

I'm home, but the heat is gone. No fire, no warm room, no burning kerosene lamp.

At the Bot, my old college house, some would say we had people over to warm the place in the winter. We didn't call them housewarming parties, but maybe that's what they really were. Just to raise the temperature a degree or two.

In late summer, the stifling air would rise and ripple. Humid, it would stagnate in the tiny living spaces that honeycomb the second floor. I remember how small my room seemed then. I couldn't turn around without bumping into something—my bed, my dresser, the boxes of stuff I hadn't unpacked. Heat makes things expand. The Bot was enormous, but restricted me at every turn. No air-conditioning. No insulation or decent windows to keep in any cool air.

During those hot months my six roommates and I would leave the house at night to find some relief from the stagnant air. Piling into two cars, we called friends and classmates to join us at Lake Padden. We went along the unlit trails. Parked cars, dense forest, and a dock suspended over the oily black water reflecting moonlight. We'd strip and leap without question, no longer adults. We were skin, hair and feet. Below the surface we felt the pressure of the lake curl around us.

Now I'm in the house watching my breath with every exhalation. I think I'll wait until the warmest months to return to Lake Padden—when the crowds are out and families sprawl on the lawn, the docks reserved for sunning teens—with friends that, hot and cold, have found space, relief below the surface.

The Cold Season

Would you believe I've been looking
for rain, here, with few days remaining
in this fleeting season of summer?
Our days are numbered that we might
share with the sun in a clear blue sky
and the hours growing warmer,
and I have kept an eye out for the clouds.
Only I wish for the conditions and doubt
that might send us all deep inside
our dark homes to sleep and read and pray
in preparation for the coming colder days.
Would you believe that the sight
of slate gray spanning horizon to zenith
and down is one I am quite taken with?

Ordinary Time

Summer, yet with missing
heat. I try to be listening

for cancer, suicide, for farewell
at the lakeside memorial

where we stand shore-side
watching brother baptized

in joy and grief. We weep,
each of us, as creeds repeat;

it looks too much like giving up
disrupting what is left of us,

how our calendar ends in flames
like tongues of fire, and names

I muddle with unholy words.
Everything I thought I heard

is wrong. My ears are not
what they used to be, what

they still should be—and
at my age, no less. Ran

a knuckle along my chin
to stop the cold itching

drip of latent empathy
caught sideways in the breeze

and indignation. This June
we anticipate to resume

from our water sacrament,
Messiah, one who was sent

to keep us from all this death.
This June, we hold our breath.

Oregon Hotel. On the lake,

even with the hearth
left cold, there is smoke
in the shelves and between
the sheets. Blankets
worn in time by weary
men and women on
vacation with their children
or alone; fabric
threadbare by the toss
and turn between
days on the lake or hiking
Hells Canyon. Rustic
and remote, out of doors
tourist attractions
where one might live as in
old westerns. Scotch
and bourbon whiskey
served on rocks or neat
on a heavy lacquered counter.

The Backwoods

There the fiddleheads reach
upward. Air ambles
in fog and pollen and
imprints left around
the roots of giant pines.
They call you
back, if you're listening:
moans, grunts, or wails,
like something roams
between the trees and
leaves tufts of hair for us
to find and follow back,
far into the forest.
The stories go further back.

Sound & Vision

1.

Everything I could want to know
I learned from David Bowie,
space cadet   alien
the thin white duke
of glamour
rock and roll

2.

my heart beats me
          against the drum
of my ear more than it
          used to and it's
been hard to hear
          since

          we shouted over
the opening act
          and my head didn't
ache the way it does
          when conversations
carry

and bleed their ways over
          into ours and I
rub my finger through
          my ear canal
and try to hear
          you

this is because of that
electronica show where
    I stood too close to stacks
of amplifiers and
    danced until the shock
broke

my tympanic membrane
    which later slid off
my lobe and into
    my hands while
I stood singing in the
    shower

3.

sometimes, I wonder what makes a man
act onstage and sing and dance, painted,
and make of himself a spectacle, to be seen

sometimes, I wonder what it is he sees

4.

my bad eye
and its brother lie
they refuse
visible truth
and instead
choose to blend
my poor sight
too tired for
anything but blurs

5.

David, I wonder
about sight
and noise
and whom I might blame but
myself for
losing both,
about the fist
in your eye
that keeps it dilated
and the voice
in your throat.

To Helena, once again

the bellows are blowing with force
I am still surprised to consider ferocious
for how long I have weathered them here.
They say it has rushed along
the coast, down from the Alaskan cold—
this chilled edge we have to summer.
Nearly, I went over the edge, I
am ashamed to admit, taking offense
at the nip of wind, as it mussed my hair.
Surprising, this chip on my shoulder,
you know. That is, you'd understand.

Zuanich Point

Looks like July is clouding over
and keeping the sun all to itself.
We try to laugh as we watch it leave
like paper embers caught in updrafts,
pretending we have forgotten
how love is tearing over in the lids
of old men whistling on porches
between drafts of tea and lemonade.
We remember seasons because they pass.
This one seems to keep us guessing;
on the edge of our Adirondack chairs,
eyes to the horizon for the spectacle
and solitude, positioned north and west,
for a better view as summer sun sets.

III.

The Cup

A fortune teller might read the coffee grounds in the bottom of this cup like finely milled tea leaves, but not me. I sit at a table for two, with some of the best coffee in town and a steady rotation of companions: mentor, friends, roommates. The coffee gets me out of bed, the company brings me here; yet however important the person opposite me truly is, I cannot help but drift.

Lately, I've been the mere suggestion of a body, my senses rendered vacant, as though the nerves in my mouth and nose and eyes and ears have been hollowed to straw. I'm only vaguely conscious. All the while, I hover over my drink, hoping it will quicken with its heat and smell. The fidgety feeling of caffeine makes me think I should drink it less.

Recently finished with college, I'm sure I've missed an important lesson concerning how one manages to actually live a life. I want to ask everything I should expect for the future. I want to ask if love and marriage are paramount, if one can actually be so devoted. I want to ask what it is to be twenty-five and married, thirty and single, fifty and divorced, and so on. I want to ask if writing and music should keep any space in my life at all. I want to ask if I should look for a job other than bookseller. And I want to ask about faith, about how Christianity lately seems so inconsistent and hyper-political and simplistic and baffling all at once, and why I should care about a spirituality that demands my whole life.

I want to ask, but I don't, afraid I don't want to know the answers. Afraid the answers will only spawn more questions. More afraid no one has answers for me, I take my cup instead and drink. The coffee is lukewarm and I think about the Revelation of Jesus Christ: *Would that you were either hot or cold*, he says, *but that you are lukewarm, I will spit you out of my mouth.* For whatever it's worth, this tepid coffee is mine. I go for another draft and another, until the cup is nearly empty.

Each day feels like an echo. The bay smelling mild as tap water. Sunlight slanting through the café window, screened by translucent frost. Eight other conversations dulling to murmuring.

The snow falling outside mutes the world. I tilt my cup to swirl its contents, watching the detritus of coffee grounds twist like a quiet hurricane, attending abstractedly to my companion at the table, and wondering if the growing pieces inside me, larger and heavier by the day, might, in time, develop a certain equilibrium.

My mind turns to Jesus and his cup, in the divine hours at Gethsemane, knees bent, chest heaving, sweat cresting his brow growing darker and darker.

How bold of me to compare my apathy to his agony, my uncertainty to his suffering. Still, I want to ask, *Father, would you remove this cup from me, this tepid cup.*

The Other Son

The prodigal was never the problem, I think. The spite,
  the bitterness wasn't because the
lost being found warranted celebration. Indeed, I stand with
  open arms to the one son's
return and might even join the festival were not the father's
  attention to the other son so
cavalier. *You are always with me, and everything I have is yours,*
  a rebuke
for having never taken advantage, for waiting in bated hope and
  expectation for a simple
and singular token given from adoration and not coercion. So
  vogue, now, blaming the
father.

Christmas Morning

Almost, I didn't wake up,
and felt worse for wear.
I was so close to being swallowed
entirely by blankets and comforters
I never asked for but wrapped
around me anyway.

When I rose, I began
with sacred words mumbled
by unmoved lips and foggy head,
an insincere act meaning well.

To myself, I am
a person always out of breath,
quietly and leisurely being
driven out of my mind. And you
still regard me with a nod,
a smile, and a pleasant hello.

Because I speak on my feet

the tongues of my shoes slide to the side
the way my tongue slips aside
to almost say what I mean
like when I forget to use consonants
to say I love you   it instead slips out
I
   O
     U

and I close my eyes and try
to imagine I can't understand
what people say
what
     you
       say
like switching my brain to world radio
pretending I'm the only one
and no one can scale my language barrier
to return to a time
before I'd acquired any phrase
     to say
       to you
exactly how I've felt

a time when instead
I
   only
     knelt

On Restlessness

I've been asking myself the same question.
I know you think you want to know everything;
I would like to understand how we operate.
But I'm afraid we've both been losing sleep.
Come morning, we'll step onto the floor
with no more than a yawn, stretch, or a blink.

I won't have the time it takes to blink
before today has again stifled any question
that might hinder my progress across the floor.
And now you think that I know everything,
for the nights I spent your waking hours asleep.
This is simply the only way I can operate.

Suppose revolutions weren't how days operate.
Suppose we relied on how often we blink
to decide the time between waking and sleep.
I don't think we would have any question
about the sun, zoology, God, and everything.
We'll spend hours charting stars, backs to the floor.

When you can make angels touch the floor,
there will be nothing left to manually operate.
The universe will be in control of everything,
assuring us of this when we watch the stars blink.
What makes us anxious will be out of the question;
what has kept us up will sing us back to sleep.

Until we find answers, let's at least try to sleep.
Pull your blankets back to your bed from the floor.
If it helps, find some paper: write your question.
Mine merely asks *How do you and I operate?*
I wrote it when my hands were numb, I couldn't blink,
and I was nervous for the state of everything.

There was never a time that I knew everything.
There wasn't a night I wanted you to lose sleep.
There are some words you can say with a blink.
There are nights I wake up curled on the floor.
There are appliances that refuse to operate.
There are solutions that don't have a question.

Today you woke with everything tossed across the floor,
from elbows thrown in your sleep—the ways you operate
that make you blink, like you answered your own question.

Compline

Awake, against the wood grain
wall, and I hear them all—the rain
drops outside. The night is full.

The steady light of a single lamp
keeps away any sleep while damp
noise at the window bids to lull

me back to bed. The comforter might
just have failed, must be a slight
discomfort in new warmth of May.

Morning threatens soon to rise;
still, I have no will to rest my eyes
or to trouble with another day.

Adequate

It's how we sing our alleluia,
how we dip body into blood
and confess, like we have spent
our last breath   and this one
has arrived by certain surprise
and is still yet quite enough
to say the least.

Slaughter Season

Before August was over, and the air remained a cotton fog in the
    lungs of all the school
chums back on grounds bleached by the heat that came
    early and stayed late,

we single-filed back through the wide stairwells and blue
    gymnasium that doubled as
the house of God on weekends when metal lockers weren't
    slamming shut

and into students, winding around the hallways toward biology
    class, or Bible—it's hard
to remember which, with the windows open and the room not
    getting cool;

the sweltering heat only made it that much harder to pay
    attention to whatever we
studied; we heard squeals across the street from animals they
    raised

at the subsistence ranch—pigs, cows, emus, and dogs at differing
    times over the
years and seasons—but, that humid afternoon kill was definitely
    a pig

because we later found the bloody stump of its neck and head,
    skinless and chewed, on
the thirty-five yard line of the overgrown football field behind the
    school

where the ranch hound took it like she'd found a new toy that
    tasted like true hide
and real blood instead of the rubber guts she was given on her
    birthday;

and, the real blood was on her snout and paws and in the yard
     and across the
parking lot, but also in the air, a thick stain on every breath that
     smelt like flesh

had come unpackaged and fissured from muscle, bone, tissues,
     and every sinew tied
together into the fabric and skin that manages to hold every piece
     together, in,

until one bullet and steel meat hooks pull the sheets apart to
     drain the blood and expose
the vital organs to elements like Idaho sky and quiet breezes from
     the south

that carried the fumes into the classroom where a girl cried while
     Mr. Syth tried to pry
us from the windows so as to discuss dissection technique—or
     was it sacrifice?

Lullaby for the Sunshine Silver Mine

"Fire Sweeps Idaho Silver Mine; Several Dead and Many Missing"
—New York Times headline, May 3, 1972

Close your heavy eyes a while,
just hear the caged canary sing
as the mountain pyre ambles by.
Fix your muffled ears on listening.

Just hear the caged canary sing
for all the widows weeping at home.
Fix your muffled ears on listening
for your breath sweeping against the stone.

For all the widows weeping at home
know now that the workers won't return;
for your breath sweeping against the stone
is all that keeps your head alert.

Know now that the workers won't return.
The canary's song, wilting,
is all that keeps your head alert,
your heart awake, and your fingers warm.

The canary's song, wilting,
echoes deep in the smothered, gravel shaft.
Your heart, awake, and your fingers, warm,
are soon undone by the anoxic drafts.

Echoes deep in the smothered, gravel shaft
calm the canaries, and mind. The Bitterroots
are soon undone by the anoxic drafts.
Unloose the strings from your bulky boots.

Calm the canaries, and mind the Bitterroots
as the mountain pyre ambles by.
Unloose the strings from your bulky boots.
Close your heavy eyes a while.

Prayers for Friends

When praying for friends and the needs
of others, we find inside us, hollowed,
there is a holy place to collect every plea.

A reservoir, a smooth, hewn, stone seam
crafted, as a rabbet joint is furrowed,
when praying for friends and the needs,

diluted in saline solution, left to seep
through oil and sediment, to where, below,
there is a holy place to collect every plea.

Anger as sacred as intercession bleeds
against the barriers we suffer to erode
when praying for friends and the needs

that linger in the diffuse hallway and mete
grievances, even still, throughout the grotto.
There is a holy place to collect every plea

we might absorb from each other, maybe,
as intinction reminds us we are not alone.
When praying for friends and their needs
there is a holy place to collect every plea.

IV

Walking the Line Backward and Forward

The oldest man I ever knew was Brother Spencer. He was 98 when he died, and I wasn't 16. In his life, he saw nearly one hundred years of the Spokane River Valley on the Washington-Idaho border. He grew up in the same farmhouse he later died in. Post Falls, where we both grew up, wasn't yet actualized when he was a child. Instead, Huetter was the major town in the area, later overshadowed by Post Falls and the lakeside resort community, Coeur d'Alene, to which a train ride cost fifteen cents.

He was a staple member of our congregation, gnarled and bent like a great oak tree out of season. His hands were enormous and spotted, his eyes kind. He sat in our church with a young couple. They had to be late into their twenties, maybe edging into their thirties, with two kids of their own. These were his grandchildren. Not the kids, the adults—his grandson and his grandson's wife. Some Sundays, when I was nine or ten, I sat next to them, operating the overhead projector during the service; I could not fathom the concept of fathering one generation, much less seeing three more.

Lately I've found myself spending more time wondering about my future. Fantasizing might be a better word. Maybe it's watching the families at church, the kids running in the sanctuary, the babies swaddled in bjorns, mother, father. Adorable Bellingham families, the kind that make your heart hurt. In these daydreams, I'm everyman. A father, a husband, I spend most of my time with my loving wife and three children, passing our days playing in Elizabeth Park, shopping at the food co-op, or visiting friends around town. I still work at Village Books, and bring home a new picture book whenever I can. But it's only a fuzzy vision. There's no life in it because I haven't been there yet.

I worked at a bookstore with a woman who had been there. She was early into her thirties and mother to a ten-year-old boy. When I told her that the Counting Crows song on the radio reminded me of junior high, she scoffed. While she was cruising with her high school pals, I was still likely wetting the bed. Later, Billy

Joel came on. "I bet this reminds you of the womb," she told me. I didn't laugh.

For someone who never gave much thought to family, outside the one I grew up in, thinking about future generations of my family makes me feel older. Then someone says, "You weren't even born when we were all listening to Billy Joel." I remember I am too young. Marriage and children are things other people do. I'm much too immature and selfish and isolated to have relationships or responsibilities like those.

At the time of Brother Spencer's death, the town of Huetter charted a population of 96 citizens. So much changed since 1904. It's hard for me to believe he never left home. In a life so long, I imagine you learn how to temper the new things with the old experiences. After a runaway wife, 5 sons, 16 grandchildren, 30 great-grandchildren, and 3 great-great-grandchildren; working on the railroad, building a church, and tending his own farm; growing older must have become a small wonder to Brother Spencer. At some point, I'd venture, he stopped paying much heed to new things.

First Cigarette

1.

As the tip of my first cigarette lit
the next and the rain soaked through
the shoulders of my new sweatshirt,
he said, *salud;* she said the same
                    in Swahili.

This instant, only facing a bad new habit
staining our index and middle fingers,
my nostrils, and the clothes we wear;
I still worried for a brother, sister, and a
                    season change

once we crush the butts against
the wet curb and all go home separate
ways and wash out the tobacco smell
in the laundry room, and use
                    a toothbrush.

2.

This is an artifact   this filter sticking in the planter
        outside our favorite pub,
slowly disintegrating in the rain   from the year I read
        noir, black like tobacco
in our old Lucky Strikes, and that night, the mood lately,
        in-patient ink, oil in the gulf,
and MRI results   and there is not enough paper to
        cover us.

3.

    years he has shown me
      how we can each be
someone strong, capable   to
    watch him quake in
      inaudible spaces
tonight and only be able   to
    watch him breathe
      in observable ways

4.

Ash
reminds me it is
Wednesday
early, and after all.

5.

Someone slips her cigarettes;
    she splits the pack in hand
      and hands them over under
        the overhang outside,

      and smiles to know
    I'm the only one who won't
    have had a chance to try
any type but Lucky Strikes.

It's while the smoke is
    dissipating that I begin waiting
      for a stranger change than one I made
        five years ago to still find

friends, faithful and kind,
expectant of the Spirit behind
and before and between every-
thing into the middle of which

I have stepped and yet feel
neither here nor there as
I prepare my leave while
praying not to slip away.

6.

Where I am going after tonight
will still smell like cigarettes,
will still rain like it is,
will still stay open late
on weekdays.

Where I am going when I leave
will still leak oil in the night,
will still test positive,
will still require medicine
for depression.

Where I am going once we're through
will not make anything okay,
will not keep us safe,
will not be better than this
lapsing moment.

My House

    walls stand
close to hold
the chill at bay
like children do,
huddled in grass
fields waiting
for the school bell.

Shaving

I carry the cloud to my face
demark its streams
as prevailing winds across
each cheekbone and down
my chin and throat
raise the sickle
from the steam in a pool
at my waist and pose
and pause in the firmament
my own face
caught in the quicksilver
and the sickle
hovers over the harvest
descends
to the scraping fields
a blade between
the age of my skin
and the new growth
along my jaw line
a little close
to smooth it over
my skin is numb
and nicked
and cool against
the torrent from the tap

Father's Day

Remember the tree house?
I suppose that was less us
than perhaps the music
at church, or the car—my bad,
bad cars. But remember anyway.

There were the grass fires
we saw when I was young.
You don't know this yet, but
I've written about them,
the smell of smoke and vanilla.

The business trips you took
us on. The short stories said
while waiting at the post office.
How you tried to convince us
that camping was fun; it was

in retrospect. The tree house,
hung from an ageless pine,
provided a new perspective
on everything I saw from ground-
level, our whole backyard.

Last Dance

I danced on your toes that night
under the bright full moon
who hung around the lawn with us
and the husks of mantis nymphs
while everyone swayed inside

> that night your brother married
> his Montana bride in July heat
> in a prairie stable west of Helena
> due east of where we last danced
> below the heavy thunder moon

on which occasion I saw your father
kiss your mother full on the mouth
as unabashed as any Protestant might
hearing news his son would soon
be married to the girl he long adored

> and now while we circled in soft earth
> I was not surprised to see your parents
> lead the floor with confident strides
> in time with *This Is the First Day of My Life*
> and laugh mirthful in the lamplight

with your sister-in-law radiant
as she cleaved to the man she loves
the rolled cuffs of his shirtsleeves
showing young muscled arms
press her in her gown to his chest

> your family now and more your pride
> as we danced until the moon was high
> you said *I wish that you and I...* and held
> a pause I filled with my lips in your hair
> and a wayward heel atop your arch

On Anatomy & Physiology

I still remember just how you look
naked, the pale curve of your back,
the quiet inlet where it bends
to meet the taper of your waist,
shower water wending where it will
along the architecture of your form.

There may have been studies of a form
such as yours, that begged charges look
and chart the firm geography they will
find around each smooth surface and back—
from the ankle to knee and knee to waist—
while changing, adapting as the figure bends,

saying, *Note where the wrist starts, thumb ends,*
and how the hip tendons each transform.
And every student might attend to your waist
but neglect the collective, assembled look
produced by the bones in your neck and back,
how they form a straight line of poise and will.

Maybe what I saw when I saw you naked will
amount to what makes or breaks or bends
me. I caught your eye, and you glanced back.
You didn't flinch or show the slightest form
of embarrassment. I remember the look—
a subtle nod and smile—you might waste

as if it were a familiar gaze, might waste
in calm, in nonchalance, in pure goodwill.
Or maybe this gaze is the way you look
into me, past the way my own body bends
to cover my soul, to hide and conform,
to be sure and have my own back—

to hold close and hold tight and hold back
like anxiety for being seen from the waist
down, naked, vulnerable, without form.
Maybe it won't matter, and maybe it will;
but, having caught you so bared unbends
me, makes me measure, take another look

at my maudlin self—a cruel look to see my back
still bends wrong, my legs, trunk, hands—a waste
of time to contest if ever I will match your form.

I have nothing memorized

1.

paper scraps tell me where I am supposed to be.
I have the answers written on my palm,
and the slick of my anxiety smears the ink,
maybe I'll remember exactly what I meant later,
about how you cross your legs so close to the hip,
how you leave your lips split in the conversation lulls:
but I have nothing memorized.

2.

ambition kills my ability to linger here.
I carry crumpled postcards
that explain where I've come from,
destinations divided by runway jets, shared armrests,
and me forgetting in-flight what I miss
about how you hold your head half-bowed before a meal
with answers in your folded fingers.

3.

I have nothing memorized that I could recite for you
upon my arrival, I will forget everything like your birthday
and your favorite place, or to visit you on lunch breaks.
I won't write you notes because I won't remember
that you like those things I forget about you,
and I will spend every day getting to know you again
and never tire of it.

Awake! Revival

And once these modern day fatigues are burned
we'll start undrawing drapes and leave them piled
against the empty bureau drawers; unfiled
manila documents; disturbed, upturned,
and potted plants; corroded lanterns; urns
that spill their contents; shattered marble tiles;
and hardwood planks misshaped and warped; all while
we dress in tails for me, and you, *couture.*

Our drowse abandoned altogether there
is left to blaze along with everything;
and, we in motorcade display arrive
atop the high-rise over everywhere
to see the beacon light and rising string
of smoke from our unraveled former lives.

Conversation Piece

"We're not going to Vegas!
Because it's tacky, and
I want to get married,
not hitched. I want a big
chapel with chandeliers, not
cranberry velvet and neon lights.
An ordained minister will perform
the ceremony with a suit and tie,
not a washed-out rock-star
wannabe with rhinestones and sideburns."
You said this.

"If you truly love me, then please
don't ask for Vegas. I want
everyone to hear the story of
us, and when I put our wedding
photo out on the coffee table,
I want people to see us
and not Sin City. I don't want our
marriage just to be a conversation
piece. I want romance, I want
my father to give me away
when I take your name.
If you truly love me,
you'd do this."

You said this,
not 12 months ago,
and now we meet again
after parting ways, after
you broke my heart when
you slid into the crooks
of his open elbows.

You're at the local Hitching
Post, all flowers and white veil,
the county courthouse across
the street, and I don't see
anyone who truly loves you.

On Province

Tell me what you remember
about normal school, in 1884
near Limousin, the region
where the valley dips just
below the continent, or so
you said you once thought.

Tell me what you thought.
How often did you remember
to write to your family so
they might not worry? Four,
five times a month, or just
once in a while? A region

as remote as that region
didn't get a second thought
from the postman, just
a trip when he'd remember
the stacks of letters sent for
the girls, the children, so

many of the faculty, so
lonely in that French region
that year there were four
months of snow. The thought,
I'm sure you remember,
still turns your mood. Just

tell me what you might adjust.
Tell me how you might sew
together stories you remember
for nights when the entire region
remained home, deep in thought
over what the rolling plains are for

if they are buried nearly four
feet under snow, in the unjust
turn of winter, as if, they thought
the earth itself had forgotten so
quickly our cattle raising region.
Tell me what you remember.

I never thought of snow before;
now it's all I remember. Tell me just
how we survive so remiss a region.

The Long Saturday

Today, I remember that you died.
Not how or for how long, just
your momentary brush with mortality,
a dull epoch emerging with your exhale.

Since the dark, early morning I've known
your absence and your promise
to return, devoid of faith enough to decide
which is easier to accept completely.

Each hour elapses, and nothing
resolves except the quickness of unbelief.
You wither in my mind just as your body
before you, and my hope before that.

Suppose night remained, weeks passing
only in shadows and snow; and, days
hesitate, clouds sustain today's grief.
And here, fearful and fitful, I rest.

The hypochondriac floats

rumble aside vibrant July sidewalks
in a small town parade. I overhear
a woman say, "Fireworks don't
last that long." You told me
the same thing.

A Restoration

Ochre bathroom cabinets
sold in sets as if antique
storage space were limited
only by the dust it's kept
years too long. The shelves begin
showing age when cleaned with cloth
doused in polish, oil, or stain.
Slats, untouched for decades, weep,
sagging under all the strain
to maintain what age has stripped.

The Way Leaves Age

Here the trees are rusting just
a little sooner than last year, a little
brighter shades against the clear
blue sky. The way the leaves age
and crumble away just so, and how
nothing is quite the same as this
brisk midday passed your way.

V.

Sanctuary

Growing up in a North Idaho church, I watched the men always planning camping trips and wild-game potlucks. I preferred to read adventure novels, but I sensed that real men of faith are mountain men, that to meet God it takes savvy in hunting, fishing, and blazing trails.

For how much I tried to avoid the outdoors, as a boy I conceded to my parents that I would participate in Royal Rangers, the Wednesday night program at my church—kind of like Boy Scouts, only in addition to badges for knots and woodworking, we earned pins for Scripture memorization and Bible studies. One weekend every spring, we would go camping at Farragut State Park with all the other local chapters.

We picked the same spot for our tents every year. Just in from the gravel parking lot, a stone's throw from the archery range, a short walk to the nightly bonfire. As dusk dwindled into the first hazy hours of evening, the council horn blew, and we gathered like so many aimless pups. We were led a few yards into the woods before we came to a clearing. All the boys and men congregated in a wide circle around a small wooden structure, like a miniature pagoda. The wind blew soft gusts of wilderness smells, plants, animals. I squeezed in with some of the other younger boys babbling about the next day's events—archery, slingshots, hatchets, hiking, the obstacle course. I listened, my stomach churning over the cuts and bruises I was sure to receive.

When the assembly began, there was just enough light for me to see a man crouching near the pagoda. He pulled a small box from his coat and struck a match against the edge. Just before the tip ignited, a few small sparks tumbled from the point of friction, blinking out long before they reached the ground. He set the match inside the pagoda, against the kindling. Soon the smell of crackling pine mixed into the breeze that filtered through bushes and branches. Somehow the circle seemed smaller, the shifting flames pulling even the furthest faces closer. Night wrapped around us, but we were bound around the fire.

A shiver climbed my spine as we sang. I was mesmerized by the glowing embers, the steadily crumbling structure of firewood. Maybe I felt the presence of God: for that hour, I rested from the anxieties I harbored toward the activities planned for the rest of the weekend. But when the fire went out, I succumbed to them. I cried—and convinced my ranger leader to take me home.

I don't understand why God loves me, someone who finds fulfillment in words and music over hunting and camouflage and sports, and too often feels disconnected because of it. Still, over a decade after I wept my way home from camp, I enjoyed a weekend retreat in Leavenworth, rafting the Wenatchee River. Somewhere along the rushing mountain run-off, I resonated with the muggy, abrasive air and sharp, striking water. And it seemed to me that perhaps God is in the wilderness, and the tabernacle choir, and everywhere in between.

Divide Wisdom, MT

Along the divide, the storm
began, as sky blue slipped to
slate haze before my eyes.
Then, there were only hills
and highway—me, alone,
southbound, thinking aloud,
unsure the taste of words.

The imagined conversation
clouded me more than any
we'd ever actually shared. By
now I might not recognize
a thought of you rooted in
the truth. And I fear the sun,
for when I left, it broke above.

Out of Ink

My pen slides along each page,
lifting at the end of each word,
but only sometimes between the letters,
meaning slipping in and out of ink.

Elementary school taught me
to write in print and then in cursive,
words in casual and formal wear
that spill out left-brained stigmata.

I remember desktops with sketches engraved
deep in their wood which sometimes
possessed my writing when the paper
overlapped against the creviced surface,

when I was given handwriting assignments
with letters to trace like connect-the-dots
on wide-ruled paper. The grooves
worked in opposition to the tracing lines.

I entered high school in 2001,
a small private academy in a small,
private town, where the teachers
loved the way I looped my l's,

each curve leaning to the right of the page
like my scripts made advances
in civil handwriting rights,
where all letters are created equal.

The Chimera

My name is Samuel Francis Gray,
born to parents expecting twins.
Beneath the chandelier they
persist with this christening gown
and baptize the only child left.

Father, raise the hem of my lace;
Mother, shed a tear as they
drip holy water down my face.
Cry for my brother; he never came,
though he's nestled in my body clefts.

I remember he died before
he had ever lived, but I
gained him in the womb.
I was born with his bones
and heart and lungs and eyes.

And I will fall in love
with Henrietta Mills;
and his will be the eyes to see
and his heart will pound my ears
to feel the flush of fidelity.

As two, we three will join as one,
until Henrietta's heart halts
and my brother's splits along—
quartering the ventricles from
the aorta, from each atrium wall.

Alone, but for my brother's parts,
his lungs breathe in fits and starts
his eyes that no longer see his love.
When Henrietta dies, my brother will fade,
and I'll be left to live slumped from his bones.

St. Peter's Hospital Nursery

Wounds our wombs could keep away
rest against the skin while our mothers pray.

Inside, we regard safety as a cage
crafted from flesh, from sinew, from faith.

I delayed for ages to desert this place,
afraid of every cut and bruise and break,

unaware that the body kills this strange embrace
unless relinquished—made to evacuate—

and I am foreign to my released shape.

Mother's Day

1.

Ear close to the sounds
in your throat, reverberating
through the muscles of your shoulder.
How I hear *Jesus, Jesus*
and sleep again, after waking.

2.

Sunup and your eyes
are tired. We are the road
between home and home.
Visiting grandma, and coast,
a host of other relations, I
almost prefer the time
between.

3.

Skin like mine is fragile.
Skin like yours has learned
to take care of itself.

4.

Here, I rest, soundly, humming
my way back to bed. The roads
between us are appreciated for
how they connect.

Song of St. George

Near foot of barley hills and roads
rides fair Penelope
across the pasture by the church
with George, on faithful steeds.

Within the guarded bulwarks' hold,
the Presbyter and priest
consoles his wife and eager waits
the day they are released.

The ruined walls of belfry stalls
all crushed beneath the feet
of dragons dealing blows to stone
and wrecking their new keep.

The saint strides out against the wind;
his foes crawl forth to meet.
He draws his sword, the dragons arch,
their fire shirks his shield.

And George, before the raided church,
is scorched in harsh defeat,
as willows wail their mourning song
for old-time jubilee.

The daughter of the Scotch Reform
looks on at all the grief
with furrowed brow and prayerful heart,
the Lord her soul to keep.

She begs the Lord to raise her knight,
commissioned to relieve
her parents from the monsters' clutch
and tortured devilry.

The hero fell in bitter brawl
with ancient sorcery.
The serpents crushed him once and twice,
will gladly make it three.

Below the boughs of weathered yew,
he lies revived in sleep,
from fiendish claws and wicked wind,
from monsters' flame and teeth.

Again he rides toward church and snakes,
again their fires breathe.
Their heads brought low to seal his fate,
his sword is plunged in deep.

The demons' scaly necks are hewn
by blade, the cut is neat.
Decapitated, now their forms
lie, mountains in the wheat.

Without their fearsome dragon guards,
the captives are released,
are reunited with their girl
whose suitor felled the beasts.

"Inspect the carcasses, ensure
that each, true in defeat,
will never terrorize the land!
So, spark the revelry!"

Good Father cries in triumph song,
a celebrant decree:
"We'll stack the pyre high and wide
and burn our enemy.

"Let's sing and dance and raise our glass
to God and George and sweet,
Penelope!" The fire blaze
builds fast and quick and free

while men and women, children, run
to join and dance and leap;
but, George bows out and slips away
into the sanctuary.

He crosses head and shoulders once
and slides down to his knees.
A single prayer before he climbs
above the tower frieze.

And from the steps he looks out on
the rolling prairie fields,
the celebration, kith and kin.
He watches, guards, and keeps.

Lent

Tomorrow is Ash Wednesday, and
I am already empty.
Soot shrouds my brow, evenly,
a note left by a soul lent
to a warden who didn't want it.

Call me brother. Console me
with a gentle grip on my shoulder,
or slap me on my back and knock
a small, fragile fragment
of faith or hope or love loose.

I've given up so many things.

Sunday Morning Bread

How can the guests of the bridegroom
mourn while he is with them? —Jesus of Nazareth

Sunday morning bread and tea with cardamom,
a table set with dishes and us gathered round,
clutching hands, praying for the kingdom come.

There are tissues trailed about the table from
soggy eyes, blown noses, and open mouths
served alongside bread and tea with cardamom.

Everyone glares at Grace, sitting deaf and dumb
at the corner of the table while we sit and shout,
clutching hands, praying for the kingdom come.

From where we sit we cannot see the sun
and we weep and wail at the grieving clouds
covering Sunday bread and tea with cardamom

while we refuse to even taste the honey
or any food before us, and instead doubt,
clutching hands, praying for the kingdom come.

We gnash our teeth over these wasted crumbs.
We starve ourselves at the table set out
with Sunday morning bread and tea with cardamom,
clutching hands, praying for the kingdom come.

Against Acedia

Did you, by kismet, see the sky tonight,
its pallid stripe above a glowing frame,
the bound horizon, halfway held by light
and halfway sunk below our Boundary Bay?

Might you have noticed in its gloaming way
from mild, July translucent haze, the crisp,
deciduous, great silhouettes against
the firmament in darkened foliage trysts?

The noonday demon, cooled to tepid lisps
incomprehensible enough that we
can pause and hear the widened leaves all hiss
above his fervent muttering ennui.

Rejoice, again, my tired, doleful soul.
Rejoice, yet, even while tonight grows cold.

Chernobyl Convalescent Home

I'm much more like Chernobyl than you'd think:
sleeping years, ending days in unfamiliar space,
waking up at night to look the mirror in the face.
The bomb went off with all I knew in a blink,
leaving my past crumbling down, a ruinous stink.
But I was younger then and could find a place,
find a new beginning at a quarantined pace.
Now I'm older and ready to give in, to sink
into the dirt and spend my last few years—
retire in the contamination so contentedly.
I'm old enough to die: I'm old enough to brave
the risks in the ground still radiating nuclear.
I want to be home for what's left of me,
to rest in salvation of what I could not save.

Eschaton

Strange the way the moon pulls the earth and its anatomy, along
　　　the rotation of days,
and leaves my running trail air stale and expiring. We watch the
　　　sky for signs that our
time here is over, or ending, because of our age, because we are
　　　tired of everything we
have made. We wait for a single tidal wave to refresh, restart the
　　　earth, so maybe all the
old things will be new, so that maybe the pulling against our
　　　limbs and coastlines might
settle toward stillness and we can finally rest.

Acknowledgements

First, to L.L. Barkat and Marcus Goodyear, without whom this book would not exist. And to those at *TheHighCalling.org*. To my family, always loving, always supportive. To Ansel, Ben, Bobby, Jake, Lorin, and Seth, my family of friends. To AL and MT, to Jacob, to Christine, to Emily, to the Goodwins, how wonderful you are to me. To Lisa and Abbie, my writers group. To Jim Schmotzer, to Seth Thomas, mentors and role models. To Oliver de la Paz, Brenda Miller, Roberta Kjesrud, Jeanne Yeasting, Don Anderson, Jake Tucker, Ryler Dustin, Graham Isaac, Robert Huston & Poetry Night Bellingham, Jory M. Mickelson, and David Hoskins, actively making me a better writer. To Susan E. Isaacs, Karen Spears Zacharias, Carol Cassella, Mary Guterson, Sarah Cunningham, Justin McRoberts, Renee Johnson, Jordan Green & *Burnside Writers Collective*, Village Books, Elliott Bay Book Co., *Jeopardy Magazine*, *The Penwood Review*, *Chronogram Magazine*—writers and networkers, encouragement and inspiration, editors and literary reviews, support all around. To the INN, and to First Presbyterian Church, Bellingham.

Also from T. S. Poetry Press

Barbies at Communion: and Other Poems,
by Marcus Goodyear

Marcus Goodyear's poems are portable, easily carried in the
mind, tightly compressed and deceptively simple, like a capacious
tent folded into a package you can tuck in your backpack.

— John Wilson, Editor, _Books & Culture_

From Barbies to tea bags and credit cards, from broken pipes to
communion wafers and mowing dead grass, Marcus Goodyear
moves us through our world. His juxtapositions of the conven-
tionally sacred and profane reveal to us the falsness of our
conventions. Where the vision is large, all is sacred.

— John Leax, author _Tabloid News_

God in the Yard: Spiritual Practice for the Rest of Us,
by L.L. Barkat

Mix Richard Foster and Annie Dillard in a blender, and you'll
pour out _God in the Yard..._

— Ginger Kolbaba, editor Christianity Today's _Kyria_

L.L. Barkat's wise words move us more deeply into matters of
consequence.

— David Naugle, author _Reordered Love, Reordered Lives: Learning the
Deep Meaning of Happiness_

Available online in e-book and print editions